Chez Pétrouchka

John Surowiecki

Bass Clef Books
Cecilia, KY

First Edition

ISBN

978-1-312-34219-4

Cover Art

Petroushka's Room
Alexandre Benois

Bass Clef Books is an imprint of MARZEK Publishing
Mick Kennedy, Publisher

Printed and distributed by
Lulu.com

$12.00

Contents

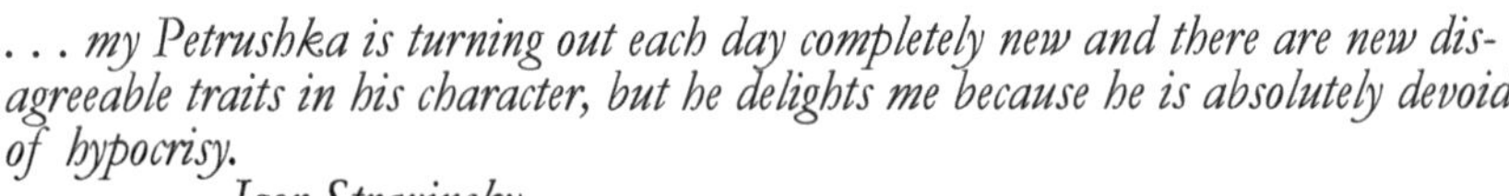

. . . my Petrushka is turning out each day completely new and there are new disagreeable traits in his character, but he delights me because he is absolutely devoid of hypocrisy.

—Igor Stravinsky

For Shap

Special thanks to George Drew and the East-West Writing Group, Storrs, CT

I.
Enter Pétrouchka

PUPPET SAYS BEING BOOTED ONTO STAGE IS A KIND OF BIRTH

Am kicked in the ass which is to say am born
somersaulted into this given

that keeps on giving. Am obliged to call
offending buttkicking shoe dad:

or mom: or either: or both.
Am a bastard in any case:

unwanted: unnecessary: not alive except
that Pétrouchka moves: speaks: thinks.

Am here alone: not a creature stirring:
no ceiling no floor

only the abyss above
and the abyss below:

solid vaporous liquid colloidal:
black matter lives:

Am Pétrouchka apparently: puppet of rags
and *papier-mâché:* rage and mucilage.

Am obliged to wear motley: a jumble of patches
each with little red cats and dogs:

little red choochoo trains:
red circus tenttops: pennants flying.

Am fleshless mumu fabric
minibolt of felt *mademoiselle's* charming chiffon.

Am what the ragman uses to dab his syphilitic scabs.
Am basic A line with bib *à la* Montaigne:

cuffs with red flowers
that grow nowhere on earth.

Have puffy buttons: have a voice
which can be cleared: ahem ahem.

Pétrouchka sings for moms and pops and kiddos
but speaks for Pétrouchka only.

Am minutes old and already weary:
have nothing to base anything on:

nothing to compare anything with: or to: or against.
Am neither living nor dead. Am lively but inert.

Am bonedry drycleanable bloodless lymphless.
Have a skeleton made of kleenex.

Am heartless or have a hollow heart
or a heart filled with *merde.*

Am lungless spleenless liverless.
Am missing islets of langerhans.

Am not handless however. Have red blinilike mitts
flat floppy thalidomidic paws: ulnausurping

worthless little flippers: can't hold crap:
ergo: Pétrouchka is quick to hug: everything.

Embrace the all. Embrace the embrace.
Always comes up emptyflippered.

Am the size of a dick
but have none: maybe one

will soon take root.
Will watch for it: you too.

Am sadly clownish:
longnosed toothless

tongueless and yet Pétrouchka speaks:
testing 12 3 4: has a voice anyone can hear.

Am barely solid: barely anything.
Am lacking in gray matter.

Am eyeless in gauze: sans vitreous good humors.
Am not without vision.

Am footless and fancyfree!
Am lacking toes: Achilles tendons too!

Pétrouchka feels cold all right
but never gets cold feet.

Pétrouchka paces like a caged panther
or glides atilt through the air like a hawk.

Am home to major constipationist forces:
rumbles in the jungle:

something huge stuck up Pétrouchka's ass: plugging
freakishly commodious anal cavity

all the way to the brain. O the mind swoons:
flips and flops: turns itself about.

Am without amenities. Don't eat: can't eat:
mouth sewn shut: line of burnt umber crayola.

No start no finish no duodenum no intestines
no bladder no guts no glory.

Am serf sans turf in the middle of Moorgicland:
Moormagician in command of the forces of Nature:

Pétrouchka in command of the feces of Nature.
Am a sorry waste of the universe's time.

Am mean and vulgar and small-minded:
am ignorant and don't know why:

a priori and *a posteriori* ignorant:
ignorant of what makes ignorance.

Am a favorite of kiddos who sing kyries
on the laps of priests.

Am an evil seed in the loam of young minds.
Maman et Papa: give the family a treat!

all week every week:
halfoff for kiddos: little elves of evil:

cruel and intolerant: selfish and immutable.
Am an unwise fool: bleed ragu of rags.

Have single tear painted where love tears begin.
Wear a pointed hat with a puff on top:

Pétrouchka lives in the cubism of night:
shadows laughing: all laughter is elegiac.

Am friendless. Am lost when found. Am fucked.
No: no dick still. Thanks for asking.

II.
Pétrouchka Addresses the Audience

Pétrouchka who doesn't hate anyone on Earth
doesn't like you.

At least you pay to show kiddos a good time.
PENNIES POUR INTO PUPPET'S POCKETS!

Am always aware of you: face to faces through
fourth wall fifth wall: wall to the $n^{th.}$

Stop drooling please. You need to listen.
You need to shut your pieholes.

Am 7/8 despising
1/8 tolerating you.

Stop whispering into the little seashells
of kiddo ears as if you knew something.

PUPPET CLAIMS ADULTS DON'T KNOW SHIT
And stop pretending you're enjoying yourself.

Am wondering why you laugh
at poor tattered Pétrouchka.

Tears of guffawing?
Sidesplitting suffering?

In reality Pétrouchka is doing ok:
your basic ordinary problems: ups and downs:

bills to ignore debts to accrue investments to raid
ATMs to empty: usual crapola.

Success eludes: faith deludes: despair intrudes.
What is life? Probably prolegomenon.

Am Pétrouchka nonetheless.
Am without social graces.

Am unlovely to look at:
star of stage screen and shithole.

Am alone in this chez dump: somewhere
someone is dancing: *Elle avait une jambe de bois!*

You: audience: rows of faces: young old:
pissing pants: glued to phones.

You clap hands whistle hoot.
Moms 'n' Dads: kiddos will no longer obey you.

Even now they doubt you: laugh at you:
prey on your wishfulness:

spit lungers all over your Cheerios.
How soft you are: how easy you are to betray.

Kiddos already videokill with AR15s: rat a tat tat tat:
survival among animated trickster gods.

Am Hermes Dolios springing on mercurial feet
teaching art of dirty tricks. KIDDOS CHEER

III.
Ballerina Dances for Pétrouchka

She's called beautiful by those who don't know
what beauty is: am talking about you: adults

desperate for loveliness: look at you
adoring the rosy smudges of her cheeks

the wet red triangles of her lips:
her glass eyes and dowelpunched dimple

waxy skin and brassspun hair.
Makes you stain your pantaloons.

PUPPET MAINTAINS DIGNITY THRU IT ALL
Am quick to see what a skank she is at heart:

a creature of *schmattes:* detrituspaste hardened over time:
motheaten tutu and plastic tiara:

and a camisole tanktop in pink:
holding nothing: *la grande prairie.*

Am no stranger to the cheesy and unsightly:
will not turn away:

will not point fat hand:
will not say a word.

Pétrouchka sees her offstage waiting for her cue:
cool remote: ice puppet.

Then am looking at something very strange:
something unlike anything Pétrouchka knows.

Ballerina has feet! What the . . . ?
She has slippers with ribbons: rigid toes:

Pétrouchka is all curtain down there: subsublunary:
she dances on the night: darkness is her floor.

And look up: something more than night sky:
strings grow out of her: gossamer threads:

when she dances it's all over folks:
herkyjerky extravaganza.

O am a goner: Pétrouchka is dizzy as a *pijac*:
worldshifting skyspinning: brain races at panic level.

All to a tune kiddos whistle: la la la la la la la:
her few steps astound: Am touched beyond
comprehension.

PUPPET CONFESSES LOVE FOR BALLERINA
She glides: a breeze from the Indies.

She leaps and floats: a kite made of moondust.
She turns left and the world turns left.

She pirouettes and the world spins off its axis.
She hangs in the air: *pas de cheval pas de poisson*

pas de chat pas de whole goddam zoo.
Her stuffing turns into gold lamé: stitching flawless.

She transcends common cloth: free: empyrean.
While a hand continues to reach up Pétrouchka's ass.

Pétrouchka launches flood of overwrought adjectives.
Ballerina turns: whispers to kiddos: conspiracy: aha.

Pétrouchka is now a joke they share:
kiddos are screaming with delight: little fuckers.

Am drowning in an ocean of jeers and sneers.
With every pirouette she talks trash

about Pétrouchka: what a jerk:
what a buffoon: what a schmuckatelli.

And Pétrouchka can't answer back: no retrash.
Say something ugly and sweetness comes out.

Am creating an ocean of honey: lugdunamean sea:
waves of laughter.

Am alone with countless kiddos: moms: dads.
All gone mad with laughter.

They mock Pétrouchka: poor poor poor Pétrouchka:
dickhead without a dick.

IV.
Exit Ballerina

Have decided to dance: for her:
ignite dancer's passion through dance.

Am swirling now: cyclonic meteorological episode:
then anticyclonic: then kinetic insanity.

Am cantastoria of chaos: just for her:
moving in all directions: all at once.

Am out of control.
Kiddos are now superdelirious with joy.

Pétrouchka thrown around the stage by Pétrouchka:
smacked wall to wall.

PUPPET ATTEMPTS BIRDLIKE FLIGHT;
BALLERINA GIVES PUPPET THE BIRD

Am soaring: worming and squirming in mid-air.
Listen: they're playing our chord.

Ballerina looks at Pétrouchka with disdain
she reserves for pigs and silverfish.

Am losing it. Have lost it.
Ballerina isn't smiling: isn't dreamyeyed

in love with Pétrouchka thinking:
O O O O: what a hot hunk of puppet:

isn't thinking she can't keep her hands off
Pétrouchka's inner mumu: and of course

kiddos want blood from a cloth.
Ballerina wants Pétrouchka

to just fucking go away. Then . . .
BALLERINA SUDDENLY EXPLODES: KABOOM:

KABOOM: pink cheeks aflame, pursed lips agape:
lashes and brows burned off: madarosis:

fingernails fall like samaras:
she loses her lips: eyes pop out

and roll into the audience: kiddos eat them:
her toes little jujubes yum yum yum.

V.
Despair

O she slithers away still alive: stage left:
takes off tutu: takes off: gotta dance:

gives Pétrouchka the old raspberry parfait:
bye bye boobah: poor poor Pétrouchka.

Keep it down you little pricks.
Pétrouchka isn't having fun anymore

and there'll be no more dancing: ever.
PUPPET TO KIDDOS: U R SHIT!

Ballerina's now a waterbaby
with bubbles forming

at her lips like silver aphids.
Or a damselfly: stunning blue and black.

Or she sinks into the underworld:
at home with Moorgician:

phake and phoney: boy wonder and wondrous boy.
No: Pétrouchka has never seen him face to face

eye to eye nose to nose rags to riches.
He dresses in rubies. His dick is platinum.

He makes money breathing.
Poor Pétrouchka Pétrouchka says to Pétrouchka's self.

Am misproportioned top to bottomless bottom.
Am gargoyle: *grottesca:* a worm at everyone's feet.

Tears flow out of every rip and rent. Am made to sob:
am born to hate what's born.

Don't laugh hideous little monkeys.
Don't say O look at the puppet

flooding the world with tears.
Logos ethos pathos: wife of bathos.

O kiddos are nervous now:
no jokes no dancing no foolishness:

no comic marvels. Now they shut the fuck up.
No peeps out of the little creeps.

PARENTS DEMAND MONEY BACK!
Up yours mom and dad.

This is what sadness is: this is what life is.
Sadness madness no more gladness.

This is your fate as well as Pétrouchka's!
Make yourselves comfortable: with grief.

PUPPET COLLAPSES ON STAGE;
KIDDOS THINK IT'S ALL A JOKE

VI.
Darkness

Am tossed into pure darkness: cold wet nighthole:
Am stepped on kicked picked up thrown down: stomped.

By whom or what? Big question mark.
Am no longer in cozy rosy Chez Pétrouchka.

Am no longer the entertainer on retainer.
Am sadly sightless in a world gone sadly blind.

Paradise relost: Pétrouchka feels like crap:
no show today or any day: no kiddos here:

no mommies daddies gramps n grammies:
no Uncle Ed: Auntie Em: no Ballerina or Moorgician.

Just Pétrouchka sinking in blueblack ink.
Life abhors a vacuum and fills it with dark.

Pétrouchka is nothing floating in nothing.
Kiddos have left the world to darkness

and to Pétrouchka: homeward bound maybe:
back to ragmen calling out: *Getch yer regs here!*

PUPPET CONSIDERS ABANDONING HOPE
Am getting the feeling darkness is where the heart is.

Darkness wants to blow Pétrouchka's nose
with the snot rag that is Pétrouchka:

stuff Pétrouchka into the pocket that is Pétrouchka:
dust Pétrouchka with the cloth that is Pétrouchka.

Pétrouchka's dick is growing:
half an inch half an inch half an inch onward!

Of limited value in a universe of one:
for Pétrouchka is now all: alone.

Pétrouchka knows nothing's out there somewhere
acting like something.

Maybe the darkness is a black rag: like Pétrouchka:
cloth to cloth: rag to rag: *une infinité de chiffons.*

Is it possible the darkness is Pétrouchka
and Pétrouchka is the darkness?

Does Pétrouchka surround Pétrouchka?
suffocate Pétrouchka? turn Pétrouchka into dust?

O how Pétrouchka wishes the dark sparkled:
but the stars have gone away: no glow Nanette:

not a ray of radium: no hope of hope.
Someone somewhere must love Pétrouchka:

and yet: every mention of Pétrouchka's name:
every memory evoking this sad dark clown

is a knife in Pétrouchka's heart: why?
They live: Pétrouchka does not: what can be sadder?

But Pétrouchka stands tall: a doily in the dark:
no longer anything to be learned

except how to live without anyone else:
how to hear silence: how to be nothing.

Must pay attention even now: look: wonder:
examine: conclude, look again.

Nothing can harm Pétrouchka anymore:
but Pétrouchka will no longer make you laugh:

laughter comes and goes and is cruel.
Am here to embrace the dark: love emptiness:

Pétrouchka is nothing to speak of
no one to speak with: no one here:

a darkness larger than Pétrouchka:
the inorganic melts into the unorganic:

a lifesong becomes a swansong sans swan:
a fibrous flutter in an eternity of cloth.

At least nothing berates and belittles Pétrouchka
or makes Pétrouchka cry molten tears:

nothing makes Pétrouchka
vomit pink chunks:

reduces Pétrouchka to nothing or minus numbers
or debrain Pétrouchka with armies of earwigs.

In darkness nothing is everything. O O O O:
Pétrouchka is in tears for all time.

Boohoo boohoo boohoo:
Pétrouchka lives with: loves: pain:

lives with: in: the dark.
Pétrouchka is hopelessly helpless.

So: bye bye immense world of delight:
hello Pétrouchka's senses zero.

Bye bye cloth: skin: big fat useless mitts.
Bye bye buttons: painted smile.

Bye bye snoteating playdohfaced kiddos:
goodbye watchful clueless *mamas i tatas*:

goodbye Moormagician:
ta ta heartless Ballerina:

ciao Maestro Stravinsky:
thanks for the notes.

GOODBYE DEAR PUPPET
GOODBYE GOODBYE GOODBYE

The cover is a rendering of Petrushka's room (*Chez Pétrouchka*) by the ballet's original state designer, Alexandre Benois—a designer for the Ballets Russes under Sergei Diaghilev who became a major figure in modern ballet and stage design. Benois's work with Stravinsky on *Pétrouchka* (he designed the set, costumes and curtain) is considered the high point of his career.

Am kicked in the ass which is to say am born
The star of Stravinksy's *Pétroucha* is a dark, nasty, long-nosed puppet, related in puppet genealogy to the irascible Punch. This work, which gives Pétrouchka a voice —vulgar and nihilistic though it is—is based on the Second Tableau of the ballet (*Chez Pétrouchka* or *Pétrouchka's Room*). The tableau opens with the puppet being born, that is to say, kicked on stage by a boot.

Obliged to wear motley
"Motley's the only wear." (*As You Like It*: II: 7: 34).

pijak
Polish for drunkard.

a heart filled with merde
Pascal: "How hollow is the heart of man and how full of excrement."

Elle avait une jambe de bois
She had a wooden leg. Refers to the First Tableau in the Stravinsky ballet in which dancers perform to the ribald song about a woman with a wooden leg.

Hermes Dolios
Hermes as deified trickster, thief, cheat, renegade and schemer.

schmattes
Rags, tattered clothes. From the Yiddish and Polish.

pas de cheval pas de poisson / pas de chat
Ballet terms: horse step, step of the fish, step of the cat.

schmuckatelli
A jerk. GI slang Vietnam era.

lugdunamean
Lugduname is a sweetening agent, 250,000 times as sweet as sucrose.

madarosis
A condition that results in the loss of eyelashes and eyebrows.

About the Author

John Surowiecki has published fourteen books of poetry. His most recent chapbook, a collection of elegies called *Missing Persons*, won the Encircle Press Chapbook Prize. Other chapbooks have won contests from Burnside Review Press, White Eagle Coffee Store Press, Portlandia Group and West Town Press. His *The Place of the Solitaires: Poems from Titles by Wallace Stevens,* was published in 2022 by Wolfson Press.

Surowiecki is the recipient of the Poetry Foundation Pegasus Award for a verse-play *My Nose and Me* (A TragedyLite or TragiDelight in 33 Scenes) which was presented by the Foundation at the Shakespeare Theater in Chicago, directed by the late Bernie Sahlins as part of the Poetry on Stage series; staged readings were also produced at the University of Connecticut and elsewhere.

Other prizes include: the Nimrod Pablo Neruda Prize, the Washington Prize, the White Pine Prize, a Connecticut Poetry Fellowship, and a silver medal in the Sunken Garden National Competition. Finally, his *Pie Man* won the 2017 Nilson Prize for a First Novel.

www.ingramcontent.com/pod-product-compliance
Ingram Content Group UK Ltd.
Pitfield, Milton Keynes, MK11 3LW, UK
UKHW021836270726
14058UKWH00002B/189

9 781312 342194